BUILD YOUR COMPANY FOR SUCCESS

RUDY SCHMID

outskirts press

Build your Company for Success
All Rights Reserved.
Copyright © 2020 Rudy Schmid
v3.0

The opinions expressed in this manuscript are solely the opinions of the author and do not represent the opinions or thoughts of the publisher. The author has represented and warranted full ownership and/or legal right to publish all the materials in this book.

This book may not be reproduced, transmitted, or stored in whole or in part by any means, including graphic, electronic, or mechanical without the express written consent of the publisher except in the case of brief quotations embodied in critical articles and reviews.

Outskirts Press, Inc.
http://www.outskirtspress.com

ISBN: 978-1-9772-1550-5

Cover Photo © 2020 www.gettyimages.com. All rights reserved - used with permission.

Outskirts Press and the "OP" logo are trademarks belonging to Outskirts Press, Inc.

PRINTED IN THE UNITED STATES OF AMERICA

Build Your Company for Success!

- ➢ Using the latest Tax laws

- ➢ Learn how to build a healthy business

- ➢ Five great ways to generate cash

- ➢ Read five amazing stories of companies with great ideas that didn't make it - and how they might have succeeded.

Rudy Schmld

Author of "America's Guide to Forming Your Own Company"

Nominated for Colorado's Top Non-Fiction Award for 2018!

Table of Contents

Part One

1. Working Capital	3
2. Cash Control	4
3. Inventory Turnover	6
4. Aging Accounts Receivable	7
5. When You Need Your Bank	8
6. Be in Charge, but don't wear too many hats!	11
7. Breaking Down the Parts of a Company	13
8. The Importance of Equity	15
9. The Income Statement and Gross Profit	17
10. Using the New 2017 Tax Changes	19
11. Put Your Ideas in Writing with a Business Plan	22

Part Two

Great ideas that didn't make it!	27
How it began!	28
I. Taxsaver	29
II. Glassbath	33
III. The Dawn of Personal Computers - - PSI, Inc.	37
IV. An Agent in Egypt	41
V. Real Estate Reports and Seminars	46
Winding Things Up	50

Foreword

If you have started your company recently, you are in for exciting times. Your mind will be filled with plans and "to do" lists as you prepare for sales and profits.

This book is designed to help you in those early days, to identify the most important ways to build and conserve cash and earn profits. I believe the helpful ideas will give you direction, and very importantly, help to avoid the pitfalls that could hold you back.

This is not a long book to read, but I truly believe it has great ideas to direct you toward success.

All my best wishes as you begin a great journey. You can set your goals, work hard, and avoid the danger areas, all helping to guide you toward success!

Part One

Working Capital

Let's take a closer look at this term, and what it can mean to you in your business. There was a technical definition used in Volume One, but I like to think of it in very practical terms. It is the cash you need to run your Company on a month to month basis, without being severely limited by a shortage of funds.

You might think of it as similar to going shopping. You may have some cash in your pocket and a credit card to back you up . You want to be sure it is enough for certain purchases you have in mind, and to buy lunch without the need of your credit card. In your business you no doubt have regular monthly payments to make, also merchandise inventory to purchase and overhead expenses of payroll, utilities, and others. If you run short of funds it may impair your credit. You want to maintain a healthy position from month to month.

My best recommendation is to use the <u>Cash Flow Schedule</u> . It is so important that I will include it at the end of this chapter. The benefit of it is, by using it regularly, it will help you to keep in mind your payment obligations, plus any new plans that will require cash payments. It is a month to month listing of every item affecting cash.

It may include increasing your inventory prior to your peak selling periods. It may include the addition of a second delivery truck. Whatever you plan as you look ahead should be listed. Of course, the most vulnerable area will be estimating your monthly sales. You will not always know what your volume will be, but as time goes by you will no doubt find it easier to predict. You will want to estimate on the conservative side to be as safe as possible. You may see a need for borrowing from your bank, or for additional investment of your personal funds. Or on the positive side, you may see a buildup of funds that will allow for additions to savings or other uses.

My suggestions are to maintain a healthy cushion in your cash planning, and build a habit of working with a cash flow schedule on a regular basis. It will give you an amazing feeling of control and ability to plan for your future.

Cash Control

As your company grows there will always be a single item that will be your key to success, and that is your cash. It is what your business is all about, to generate an ever larger flow of cash. Recently the news reported that Apple Computer had cash reserves in the billions! That amount will, of course, enable Apple to use nearly unlimited amounts for research & development of new products, and for improving the current ones. It is in a position to pay dividends to shareholders and acquire more companies if it chooses to. And, of course, larger salaries and bonuses for the top executives and other employees. That is the power of a large cash position.

Because of its importance, I feel it is worth our time to focus on the controls you will want to implement in your company to protect your cash. Depending upon your products and methods of selling, your cash will be received in a number of ways: by cash paying customers at the register, from on-line sales paid with credit cards, from checks received in the mail, sometimes by wire directly to your bank account, and by customers paying with their credit cards. All are fine ways to generate cash, as long as it is not diverted into the hands of "other people" to whom it does not belong.

I like to recall an assignment I had several years ago, to fly to Kansas City and try to solve a problem of cash shortages. It was a medium size hotel. The manager had checked receipts and believed the count was short on several occasions. I was given a room in the hotel with a table for my calculator and papers. I requested the register tapes for the past thirty days, together with deposit tickets for the same period. I noted the differences on some days, with smaller amounts being deposited than taken in. Next, I separated the employees (by their employee number on the register tapes) to isolate the one with whom the shortages had occurred. It did not take long before I was able to identify the night clerk as the one who removed small amounts regularly from the deposits.

The manager and I called the night clerk into the room and confronted him with the facts of our discovery. His only reply was to confess, explaining the desperate needs of his family. We gave him two choices: 1) return the exact amount of money he stole by 5PM that day, or 2) his theft would be reported to the police. The good news was that he returned with all of the funds he had taken. It was a very satisfying conclusion, and points to one way your money can be taken. Over time it can create serious problems for the condition of your company.

On several occasions I have seen owners prepare their own daily bank deposits, even as their company grew. While it may seem a trivial thing, something an employee could do, the owners felt it of vital importance to count their own funds and compare the total with the amount it should be.

Depending upon the method of your sales, a system can be developed to reconcile the amount earned with the amount received. For example, cash register tapes, in addition to preparing one for the customer, also maintain a cumulative total for all sales of the period. The tape can be totaled when employees end their shifts, with a new cash drawer used by the next employee. In the case of large products being sold, copies of sequentially numbered invoices should be entered in a sales journal and matched with funds received. My strongest recommendation is to study your particular selling method, and develop a plan for <u>two totals</u> to be reported that equal each other. One total is for sales, the other for funds received. When they equal each other you can rest easily, knowing you have controlled your funds.

In todays business world of highly developed technology, there are sadly many individuals who are smart in the ways of stealing. It simply becomes a challenge for them to out-smart any systems of controls in order to steal your money. For these reasons I urge you to be ever watchful of your hard earned cash. Count it yourself, or at least on a random basis to test your controls. Have your accountant review your method of controls, or even a specialist to develop a secure system. I bring this issue to your attention, not because everyone will steal from you, but because these conditions exist at an ever growing rate. With proper care and awareness you can safeguard the funds that are yours.

Inventory Turnover

This term means putting more cash in your bank account so this is a good time to discuss it.

It is a simple theory, and can be a powerful tool in your business. Basically, it refers to how long it takes to sell the merchandise you have for sale. Let's say you buy an item for resale for $100 and mark it up to $140.. When you sell it you will have earned a $40 gross profit. When you replace it and sell it again for $140 you will have earned $40 twice. If you sell the item once each month your combined gross profit will be $480 for the year. Of course, if you have five to six hundred different items, imagine the explosive profits as your inventory turns. This is the idea of inventory turnover, to keep all your merchandise moving, thereby generating cash and profits.

If you have a fairly large inventory and it moves slowly, your working capital is tied up, restricting your use of it. So I suggest you examine your specific products and determine the number of times they are sold in a month. It may require new advertising and promotion campaigns, but use every method you can afford to turn you inventory. Weed out the items that are not moving. Place them for sale to recover your investment and use those funds for the moving items. It may take some time and perseverance to determine the best mix in your total inventory, but keep in mind the potential profit increase as you improve your turnover. Learn to control it regularly and promptly. I recall my pharmacist having just one of each item on his shelves, and thought it was rather odd. The shelves almost looked empty. Asking about it, he said he orders every day, replacing everything that was sold, thereby holding his investment to the minimum.

The point to remember is to know your inventory, taking every step within your ability to increase turnover of every item. When successful, you will be amazed at your increase in working capital or, more to the point, cash in the bank.

4.

Aging Accounts Receivable:

This is simply a system of controlling the amounts owed to you by your customers. Most businesses allow customers the first thirty days to pay their bills without any extra charge, but after that the accounts are generally considered to be late. There are at least two things you can do about late payments. One is to print on your invoices that your policy is to charge interest on all charges over thirty days.

An optional method is to prepare a listing of customer balances each month in order of sale date. In that way you can easily see the number of days charges have remained unpaid. You can show total receivables by 1-30 days, 31-60, 61-90 and 90+.

Unless arrangements have been made with certain customers, special attention should be given to unpaid accounts. It may be notices in the mail, advising that old accounts must be reported to credit bureaus , or they may be turned over to collection agency or to an attorney.

You want to create a friendly atmosphere with customers, encouraging their return. On the other hand, realize that by not paying promptly, the late ones are jeopardizing your business by depriving you of working capital (the money that you should have available to you). You owe it to good business practices to protect your hard earned funds. That is why I strongly suggest the policies described above. I believe you will feel good, and in control when you use them regularly in your business.

5.

When You Need Your Bank

Going for a loan:

You have reached step one when you find the bank where you feel comfortable, where they are receptive to your business ideas. That environment will set the stage for discussing business plans with which your bank can be of help.

Now, however, you will need the right ingredients for most any bank financing. You will want to start with a plan, and support it with your business records. For example, you may be thinking of a <u>Line of Credit,</u> which is very much like a credit card. You may want use it to build your inventory prior to peak selling periods, and pay it back after your selling season. Or you might want to expand your physical facilities, possibly to add more floor space for customers, along with more warehousing. A long-term loan would better fit your needs here, say a $200,000 mortgage, payable over ten years, including interest. You might even want an unsecured loan, usually smaller than the others and for a shorter term.

Each type of loan could make good sense under the right circumstances. What that means is that it is a good type of loan for you if your plans include a clear, sound way for you to repay it. Whatever the type of loan, your lender will want to know that it will be repaid according to agreed terms.

Now, here is what is meant by the "right" banker for you. He or she will take the time to listen carefully to what you say, and try to gain a clear picture of what you plan to do. When a good understanding is reached, your banker, with the knowledge of what the bank is able to do, may offer an even better plan than you presented. Perhaps a longer term for repayment, that would reduce your monthly payments, or a better interest rate, or a higher loan to value limit (explained soon) that will allow you more cash than expected. , The end result following your discussion, will be a plan that will give you what you want and will be acceptable to the bank. That is what is meant by good banking: being able to work together to reach a mutually acceptable plan.

Now that you both agree on the goals, it will be your task to provide the supporting information that will allow the bank to carry through with its part. This is the point at which your banker might say (actually in writing) that your loan is approved, <u>subject to</u> the following terms and conditions:

- Your acceptable credit score (possibly 600 or better).

- Your past three years financial statements, or at least one if you are new in business.
- Your past three years personal income tax returns.
- A Certificate of Insurance to show the coverage you have for property and for general liability.
- A listing of assets that are available for security of the loan. It may be merchandise inventory or equipment or real estate. If real estate, it will probably be necessary to have it appraised. The bank will normally order an independent appraiser. The assets to be used are generally called <u>collateral</u>, meaning security for the <u>loan</u>.

These are the items your bank will most certainly request. There may be a few more, depending upon the type of loan you are requesting.

Let's talk for a moment about loan to value, or LTV. This is the amount of your loan compared with the value of your collateral. Let's say that an appraisal of your building offered for security is $100,000. The bank may have a policy to lend 80% of the appraised value. So that means the limit of your loan will be $80,000. The LTV is 80%. Now if you are in a strong position with your past and present records, they might go up to 85%, or in a weaker position as low as 60%. The bank's objective is to minimize its risk by having plenty of value to fall back on in the event your loan is not repaid. This is where the success of your business to date, supported by good records, will greatly help you to get what you need to carry out your plans.

Once all your material is submitted and appraisal is completed, you probably will be put on hold for a few days while the bank studies all of the data. In many cases it will mean they will prepare a "package" of your loan papers and supporting data and send it to their "<u>Underwriters</u>", meaning the committee that will approve your loan. They may have a few questions, and when satisfied, will give an approval.

The final step will be for loan documents to be prepared for your signature. Depending upon the type of loan, there could be a <u>Title Report</u>, that gives the history of ownership of your property, together with any easements or liens. Also a <u>Deed of Trust,</u> a document that describes in detail all of the conditions and terms of your loan, and what you as the borrower are committed to do, followed by what happens if the loan is not repaid according to agreed terms; also a Note that spells out the amount of the loan and terms of repayment.

You will receive a <u>Commitment Letter</u>, stating that your loan has been approved, subject to the terms and conditions in the documents, and finally, a <u>Settlement Date</u>. This will be the day you meet with the lenders, sign all the documents and receive your money. It may be a check handed to you, or a credit to your bank account. Or in the case of a Line of Credit, you will receive your authorization to draw funds as needed to create deposits to your bank account.

It may sound like a long project to request a loan, and frankly, it is. I cannot recall a simple, fast one in recent years, but it is the nature of the transaction. The banks are required to follow specific steps to meet banking regulations. The good part however, is that when you deal with the "right" bank your loan officer will try to make the process as painless as possible, will give you progress reports, and be helpful in assisting you to the end.

It is my hope that by explaining the loan procedure it will give you an idea in advance of the usual process, and show the importance of carefully preparing your records, paying bills on time and building a strong credit record. All of these steps will make it easier for your bank to approve your request.

One final note. Once you complete your first loan, repay it "as agreed", you will be preparing the stage for future financing. Each successive loan will be easier for the bank to approve. It goes to the old saying, "success breeds success".

6.

Be in Charge, but don't wear too many hats!

One of the greatest errors I made in a company that did not go well – in fact, it failed – was trying to wear all the hats. I was in charge of purchasing design, sales, financing, advertising, and every other "department".

A number of years ago I designed a clever kit to hold papers throughout the year for preparing year end tax returns. I designed it, built a prototype, found a manufacturer, financed the venture at my local bank, ordered 500 units, and arranged to sell them at my nearby drugstore.

I also prepared advertising to be placed with the display at the store. Finally, I drove to Los Angeles and hauled my kits home to be sold.

This story is described in more detail in Part Two of this book.

I did it all, with no help, no suggestions or advice from anyone. With great enthusiasm I set up my display at the store, followed by daily visits to see how many were sold. After three weeks, the manager asked me to remove them as they needed the space. I had sold a total of two kits! Why only two? They were so handy and every family needed them!

Well, that was when I began to receive advice. For one thing, the kits had been assembled using black leatherette on the exterior instead of something attractive. To tell the truth, they were ugly! Shoppers would pass them by, without even looking to see what they were.

When I finally stopped long enough to review my project, it did not take long to realize that I had been so enthused about how well my kits would sell that I overlooked carrying out my project in a professional way. While I believed my idea was a good one, I admitted that I was not a designer or a marketing specialist, or good at dealing with a manufacturer. I should have stayed with my specialty of finance and found others to carry out their specialized areas of work.

My point is not to attempt to run all departments of your company single handedly. Realize that you have certain strengths, but you are not an expert in everything. Include in your budget the cost of experienced personnel needed in your company. Sure, it will cost more, but your success may well depend upon who you have to help you run your business. Steve Jobs is given the credit for the Apple computer and cell phone, but you can just imagine the experts he depended upon to help develop his ideas? Think of McDonalds for a moment. Their burgers are good, but would they have grown to the giant they are based on the good taste of their burgers alone? A great marketing program and detailed time studies were carried out by specialists to develop the super efficient systems of selling .

You may have limited funds in starting your company, as many new companies do, but study the entire program you intend to carry out, and the specialized help you will need. Place the cost of hiring well trained people on high priority and then wait until your budget can afford them to carry it out in a professional way. In the long run, the chances of your success will be so much greater.

7.

Breaking Down the Parts of a Company

There are some exciting steps you can take as your company grows. Let's discuss some names you may have heard about companies in order to become more familiar and comfortable with them. We can follow them up with an example, to give you a better idea of how you can structure your own company if you chose to do so.

Here are a few terms relating to companies:

Entity: This relates to any organized company. Whether a corporation, partnership or an LLC, it is an entity. It is like saying you are a person.

Division: This is a part of a company, usually focusing on a special product. You might think of General Motors, with it's Chevrolet Division, Cadillac Division, etc. They may become separate corporations, but are still owned and controlled by the parent company.

Department: Any company may, and often does, divide into areas of specialty. For example, the sales department, purchasing department, parts, research & development and finance. Each would no doubt have a manager and even an assistant manager to run the activities in their department. This is the most common method of organizing a company, no matter what form it is – corporate, partnership or others.

Subsidiary: This is a company that is owned by another company, referred to as the parent company. Ownership does not need to be 100%, but must be large enough to have management control. Products sold by the two companies are often not similar. A company may be bought by another because it believed to be profitable, or to have the potential of being profitable under the new management of the parent company.

Sister companies: These are companies that are owned by the same parent. They may have completely difference products, but might benefit as sisters because the operating expenses could be shared. For example, one company might have an R & D department or certain physical facilities like warehousing that could be shared by the sisters, leading to less overhead and greater profits.

Now let's use these descriptions in an example that will help you to create an idea of how they could fit into your plans as you grow. Let's assume you have formed your company already, named "Your Name, Inc." You sell a line of bicycles. You meet Sam who specializes in motorcycles. You decide to expand your company by setting up two divisions: "Bikes R Us", with Sam as the Division Manager and "Bicycles R Us" of which you are the manager.

Sam organizes his division with two departments: the Sales department and the Parts department. You do the same, but also add a finance department. You are still in control as it is your company, and while Sam operates his division, you remain in control, meaning you can approve or disapprove decisions he makes. You can review his operating budget and give a final approval when you are satisfied with it. Sam will probably make the decisions about motorcycle inventories, but you could set a limit on the size of it, to control the amount of investment.

As you grow, your cash flow expands and you locate a corporation that carries a line of products you understand – let's say spare parts and lubricants. You believe you could increase it's profits with your understanding and management so you negotiate a deal with the owners and buy a controlling interest in the company.

You now have a subsidiary. If you were to decide to just invest in a company for a share of ownership, but without a controlling interest, you would then have an <u>affiliate</u> company. Here is one more. Let's say you did not buy any interest in the ownership of a company, but agreed to share warehousing space, thereby saving your overhead expense. With that degree of relationship you could refer to the other company as an <u>associate</u>.

Finally, you might locate a company that has more office space and warehouse space than they need. You decide to invest in the company, enough to gain operating control. Your management group negotiates an arrangement that is acceptable to share space, again resulting in lower overhead for both companies. You now control two subsidiaries that can be called <u>sister companies.</u> You have grown into the organizational growth pattern of many modern companies. I hope this gives you an idea of the options you will have as your company grows.

8.

The Importance of Equity

The definition of equity is straight forward. It is everything your company has less the amount you owe to everyone. The remaining difference is equity. In short, it is the amount you actually own in your company.

The importance of equity cannot be overstated, because it is what determines your personal value in your company. If all assets amount to one million dollars and the company owes $900,000, your equity, ownership, is $100,000.

Lets clarify, however, that in the example above, while you own $100,000 out of one million dollars, you still own 100 percent of your company. The reason is that you are the only one who owns the company, so that means 100%.

However, if others share in the ownership, whether a corporation, partnership or LLC, equity is divided among the owners. In a corporation, for example, if 1,000 shares of stock have been issued, and you bought 100 shares, you will own ten percent. The other 900 shares will be bought by others in varying amounts until all are issued. The same example applies to partnerships and LLC,s where percentages of capital are purchased instead of stock shares.

Here is a most important part of this subject. I have often observed individuals forming a company when the question arose about ownership. Without much hesitation, they reply "we'll divide equally". As time goes by, the two realize that they did not contribute equally, and that they are not earning profits equally, because one has a more responsible, time consuming job than the other. Regrets can easily grow because of this situation, sometimes proving to be fatal to the company success.

My strong recommendation is: Take time to evaluate what is being contributed by each person. For example, one may contribute land, appraised at $600,000, while the other contributes machinery and vehicles valued at $400,000. That would translate to a 60 and 40 percent equity ownership.

A second question of great importance is: "What will the profit and loss sharing percentages be? To respond to this question, I recommend taking time to prepare a job description for each. Who will be in charge and make the management decisions? What will the other party do? Once understood, decisions can be made, commensurate with what each owner will do. For example, a family partnership might be formed, with Dad as the General Partner, responsible for making management decisions, while Mom is responsible for administration. The three children perform work in delivery, as a receptionist, and maintenance. A fair division of profits and losses might be: Dad 40%, Mom 30% and each child 10%.

The percentages can be changed as conditions change, by holding a partners meeting and agreeing to changes.

There are at least four ways in which equity will change. One is by a contribution to capital, thereby increasing capital of the contributor. A second way is by annual profits, which would be added, or losses, that would be subtracted. Another way is by withdrawals, such as a cash distribution. Here is an example of how the equity section would appear:

Beginning capital	$1,000,000
Capital. contributions	100,000
Net income for year ended 2018	200,000
Less withdrawals	- 50,000
Ending capital	$ 1,250,000

I suggest giving a great amount of attention to equity, as explained above, and to any changes that occur. Think of your assets as all of the tools to assist in building profits, liabilities as the part to be diminished, and equity as the heart of your company. With a strong, healthy equity, you will possess the strength to grow; also to build your personal estate, and eventually to provide your retirement funds. Equity is the key to your present condition and also to your successful future.

9.

The Income Statement and Gross Profit

We have come to the most exciting and meaningful chapter of this book!

It is the reporting of your sales and cost of sales, leading to your profits. It is the life blood of your company, and profits earned!

I think of the balance sheet, that reports assets and liabilities, as the tools with which to operate. But it is the Income Statement that reports results! Let's take a closer look at its three parts.

The selling of your products is where life begins – it generates cash that flows into your company. The more the better! With that thought in mind, you will want to give really close attention to your products, by possibly adding similar items to your product line. Just as the fast-food companies have added salads and several sizes of burgers, perhaps your product line could be expanded in a similar way. With close study and thought, you will no doubt generate new ideas. Periodic promotions are important to stimulate consumer interest and more sales.

Take special note of the trends in selling, that is, the shifting from retail stores to on-line selling. It is far different than a few years ago, before the explosive cyber marketing came along. Malls, as much as we enjoy them, are losing their attraction in favor on on-line marketing. You will want to explore all possible ways to sell your products, possibly using a marketing specialist to help in this area.

An important step is to add new accounts to your records (General Ledger), in order to record your sales in each product category. In that way you will be able to locate your "hot" items as well as the slow ones. Reviewing the reports and comparing with prior periods will be like taking the pulse of your company. It will allow you to work toward the best mix of products, the ones with the best market appeal.

The second part of the income statement deals with Cost of Sales, the vitally important area that reports the actual cost of the products you sell. The cost of your products may have a good potential for reductions at times by earning quantity discounts or buying during promotion periods. If your products are being manufactured for you, the use of a different material might result in lower costs. By searching for a competitive supplier you might find one with a lower cost, or improved terms. You might think of this entire process as "tweaking", that is, finding small improvements that will add up to a significant savings.

When costs are deducted from sales, the all-important Gross Profit results. Your goal is to have as large a Gross Profit as you can, while still maintaining a quality product. By searching for ways to "tweak" your sales and costs, the nice result can be substantial cash in your bank account. Just as an example, if your sales were $100,000 and cost was $60,000, your gross profit would be $40,000. But if sales were to improve to $105,000 and cost reduced to $58,000, your gross profit would jump to $47,000, a welcome addition of $7,000.

The third section of the income statement lists the operating expenses – wages, utilities, insurance, and all the others that are needed to operate your company. My recommendation here is to review them regularly, comparing with prior periods, always searching for ways to hold each item from growing without good reasons. This is an area where it is easy to allow expenses to expand, sometimes greater than the gross profit.

We will reach the "Bottom Line" by subtracting total operating expenses from gross profit. This figure is your Net Income, or the final amount earned over the period being reported. It is what your hard work in managing your company is all about. While one income statement can tell you much about your results, by aligning the figures with other periods, whether monthly or annually, you will find an enlightening picture of trends. The income statement can be truly informative and exciting, providing you with the heartbeat of your company. I am reminded of companies on the stock exchange that report earnings quarterly, often causing dramatic increases or decreases in stock value as soon as results are disclosed. It demonstrates the importance of the income statement as it relates to the entire value of your company.

10.

Using the New 2017 Tax Changes

In 2017 the most sweeping changes to tax law gave us new rules for calculating and paying our federal taxes. Known as the Tax Cuts and Jobs Act, significant changes were made for personal as well as business tax reporting. The most widely applicable changes will be described here.

Depending upon your type of business, that is, corporate, partnership, etc., and your personal status, there may be opportunities to lower your taxes. By understanding the basic changes, it will give you an opportunity to plan your business and personal affairs to your best advantage. For example, a very helpful change was lowering of the corporate rate to a flat 21%. If you believe , considering all reasons, that a corporate form would be best for you, you could no doubt benefit by the lower tax rate.

Another opportunity applies to all companies. That is a completely new law that provides a 20% standard deduction of the net company profits. Although there are a few tests to apply before allowing the full deduction, it could provide a sizeable tax saving. I would suggest, because of the complexity of the calculations, that you have professional help with this step.

Let's take a look at the way in which your company income will be reported for tax purposes:

- A c-corporation reports on Form 1120, and tax is paid by the corporation at a 21% rate.
- A sole proprietorship will report income and expenses directly in Form 1040, using Schedule C. Your net income will be reported in this form together with your other forms of income, like wages, dividends, etc.
- If you operate a partnership, S-corporation or LLC, a Form 1065 is used. Within the 1065 a Form K-1 for each owner is included, identifying the name, percent of ownership and amount of income earned from the entity.

All Form K-1's are reported in the Form 1040 on Schedule E. For example, a husband and wife might each have a K-1 form, possibly the children also, and data for each will be reported on Schedule E.

On the following pages is a brief review of the tax changes, beginning in 2018. I hope they will provide you with helpful data to use in your tax planning.

Tax Rates: The first three brackets will illustrate the rates that will affect most taxpayers:

The first $9,525 of taxable income has not changed. It is 10%

The next $58,350 will be taxed at 12% instead of the old 15%

The next 97,125 will be taxed at 22%, down from 25%.

Standard Deductions: It has increased to $12,000 for individuals and $24,000 for joint returns - a big benefit if you were filing standard deductions in the past.

Personal Exemptions: Has been completely eliminated – a painful loss!

Capital Gains: They have remained mostly the same, with rates of 0, 15% and 20%, depending on the makeup of the gains.

Child Tax Credit: For those of you who have used this credit in the past will be pleased with the changes. The credit of $1,000 per qualified child has doubled to $2,000. In addition, the phase-out limit has increased substantially to $400,000 for joint returns and $200,000 for single filers.

Child & Dependent Care Credit: Has been kept in place with few changes.

Education Tax Credits: are also still in place, specifically the Lifetime Learning Credit and Student Loan interest deductions. One change has expanded the available use of funds in a 529 College Savings plan, allowing for more types of uses.

Mortgage interest: is actually the same, although lowering the amount deductible from the first $750,000 of debt, down from the million dollar limit.

A change that will hurt many taxpayers is that home equity loan interest will no longer be deductible.

Charitable Contributions: is mostly the same. The only significant change

Is increasing the limit that can be deducted from 50% to 60% of income.

Medical expense deductions: will again be deductible for amounts over 7.5% of income instead of 10%.

Deductions that will no longer be deductible: Casualty & theft losses, tax preparation fees, unreimbursed employee expenses, and moving expenses.

Pass-through Company deductions: Income earned by S-Corporations, Partnerships and LLC's will have a new break – a 20% standard deduction of the amount of income reported from K-1 forms. This new deduction was discussed above, and is referred to as the Section 199-A law.

Estate tax Exemptions: has been increased to $5.59 million for individuals and $11.18 million for a married couple, virtually eliminating an estate tax for most of us..

There are, or course, other changes that will apply in fewer situations, but those listed will be the most widely used. I hope they will be of help to you in your planning.

11.

Put Your Ideas in Writing with a Business Plan

You no doubt have dozens of ideas in mind about your company and how you will organize it. You've thought about how you will finance your operations, whether you will begin with employees, and what your goals will be. A Business Plan is the accepted vehicle with which you have the opportunity to express all of your ideas in writing. It will be a great assist to you in your own planning and of particular value to possible investors and lenders. Let's discuss what it will include and how you might prepare it.

There are templets available online to assist in preparing your Business Plan, but it is most important to realize that it should be your unique design in expressing your ideas. It can be short and concise or as detailed as you think it should be. For example, you might describe a mechanical product you plan to sell by simply referring to it by name, or go into detail about its special parts and features. I strongly recommend giving a great amount of thought to what you want to include in your Plan to best describe it to yourself and to others. Then begin with all the enthusiasm and passion you have to express yourself in creating it.

As a guide, here are topics suggested:

- The full name of your company.
- Location: the full mailing address
- Phone number and email address.
- Founders: Your full name and other co-owners, if any.
- A brief biography of each of the principals, including special education and experience to apply in the company.
- Products or services to be sold. Suggest a fair amount of detail here.
- Source of products and cost, delivered.
- Fixed expenses by month and year, such as rent, insurance and payroll.
- Financial: initial investment, borrowed funds, if any, names of lenders, terms of repayment, security for loans.
- Operations – by month and one year: Projected sales, cost of sales, gross profit, operating expenses, net profit..

- Cash flow – by month and one year: Suggest using the Cash Flow Worksheet included in Chapter 1.
- Any additional commentary you believe is important to convey a clear understanding of your company and goals.

I believe a valuable bonus in creating your Business Plan will be the confidence you will generate within yourself to carry out your plans successfully.

Part Two

Great ideas that didn't make it!

The second part of this book is filled with five real life, fascinating stories about new companies with great ideas. However, they all failed because of a variety of serious flaws.

The flaws will be pointed out and discussed in hopes that you will avoid them in your own company. As you read the stories, you will no doubt find them to be interesting and amazing for the incredible failures they suffered. Following each story, the author will comment on the success that might have been achieved without the flaws. Admittedly, they are fascinating stories, but a clear message is meant to be given about what to avoid to reach the success envisioned.

The author somehow survived following each failure, but it was not easy! His ability to move on to life after failures will be described at the conclusion of the stories.

How it began!

It may help you to understand my motivations for entering into these five ventures by giving you a brief prelude to the first company project. There were reasons for my attempts in the business world – big reasons. Let me tell you about them.

It all began in the early Sixties. This will no doubt be a familiar story that many of you can relate to. More precisely, it was in May of 1963. I was a licensed Certified Public Accountant with a solid background of preparation for my work. A graduate of the Business School at UCLA, three years with a major CPA firm provided me with good preparation for the world of accounting and business. Following those years, I decided to open my own accounting firm in the thriving community of Santa Maria, California. That was in January, 1961. My business grew beyond my expectations, leading to opening a branch in nearby Lompoc. Life was good, as I enjoyed growth with huge satisfaction.

But then came May, 1963. I met a young lady with three young children, two of them close to their teen age years. Within a short time we were married. While on a personal level I was one happy man, reality soon told me that a family of five required some serious income. My earnings as an individual provided me with a comfortable living, but now it suddenly spelled "SHORTAGE" when measured for a family of five. Three years went by and we were to add to our family with three more children, bringing us to the daunting total of eight. Food and clothing of course were basic needs, but now we were facing the dire needs of more space. Bedrooms were needed at the minimum. We were no longer a family of just a few little kids but one of major proportions. It was in these days, each becoming more desperate, that my thoughts turned to the creation of new and greater income. As I recall, there had to be an answer to quick new money. I just had to apply some thought to discovering what my new source would be.

I recall that my time was nearly fully occupied. From early morning until dinner was my office time, meeting with clients and applying my accounting skills. Evenings were filled with family activities. The only extra time I knew of was earlier than my present eight o'clock start. During the earlier hours I could devote time to something new, but what would it be? What could be developed in my mind, created, organized and operated successfully during an early hour each morning? Well, that is the content of the next chapter, covering my first attempt. Let's move on to see what it was.

I.

Taxsaver –

It began with a sudden revelation as I awoke early one morning. It would be a sort of kit in which to save and organize all papers during the year, to be used when preparing annual tax returns. As a tax preparer, this was something I knew about, a much needed item for millions across the U.S. From my experience in preparing returns, most, that is about 90% of my clients, brought their papers in a paper bag or at best, in files with all sorts of papers of various origins. It was normally part of my work to sort them , categorizing and labeling groups for use in the tax returns. Well, my kit would help and improve all that. A small file would be attached inside, labeled for categories of income and deductible expenses. Attached to the inside cover would be a listing of taxable income and deductible expenses. The kit would be shaped about like a cigar box, neatly holding all records for the year. There was even space below for a copy of the final tax return.

All of these ideas came to mind as I lay awake one early morning. It was perfect, I said to myself. Every tax paying family needs it. They can be inexpensive, easily affordable, and an obviously helpful method of saving tax records that was long overdue for the consumer market. Best of all, I calculated, I could design it, have it manufactured , sell it locally until I build a profit, and then expand the market.

With new excitement and anticipation, I drove to my office early, to begin designing. I decided the width should be large enough to hold a folded regular size paper. It should be high enough to hold an expanded file attached inside. It should have an attached cover to which the deductible expenses would be listed inside. Included in my planning were file labels and sizes of print, along with font selections. Next came the plan to build a prototype, something to prove the actual suitability of it and to demonstrate.

As a good accountant, I quickly began to put figures together, estimating the cost of a unit. This required calling to Los Angeles, where boxes would no doubt be manufactured. I brought out the yellow pages, the only source of information in those days. I talked by phone later in the morning, explained my plan and asked for cost estimates, Finally, the third company said they could make them for me. I requested an attractive Beryl wood exterior, and they replied they would call back the next day with costs and answers. With that call my excitement grew immensely, as it appeared I was actually going to be in the business I'd dreamed about. My hopes soared as I awaited the return call. I felt the costs would surely be reasonable enough to build a retail price with a healthy profit included. The next day arrived and as promised the manufacturer called. He said he had the equipment and material to build them. He had contacted a printer who could provide the files, and that he could deliver the finished product for $2.15 per unit with a 500 unit order.

Writing all this down as he talked, I was saying to myself "yes!, yes!, yes!. This would work! Finally I asked, can you get an attractive beryl wood exterior? He replied that they could not get that but would an elegant black be ok? Slightly disappointed, but greatly excited about the other information, I replied that the black would be okay. He would send a purchase order for my signature, and get working on the project. Things were actually happening!

With all my new information, I prepared a description and presentation of the project to take to my banker. I knew the bank manager well, and he was quite familiar with my accounting firm, as well as several of my clients. I showed him the prototype I'd built, also a schedule of estimated costs and proposed retail and wholesale prices, based on the cost. All of this data he understood, and said he felt I had a good pricing structure. In addition, I gave him a projected cash flow schedule in which sales of units were estimated, gradually increasing with each month. My costs included delivered costs as quoted by the manufacturer. In addition, there were estimated advertising and promotional expenses, shipping and office supplies, telephone and miscellaneous. It was well thought out, with sufficient conservatism to present a believable plan. Well, the manager studied the data and followed by asking what I would need to carry it out. Having anticipated the question , I replied that $1,500, payable over 12 months, together with interest, should be enough. Without further hesitation, he approved a 12 month non-secured loan.

Now I had the plan, the kits were being built, and I had the money to pay for it. Life was getting better. While I had no new money in the bank for my family, now I had hope, which in itself, pulled me ahead over the coming days.

A name:
During the coming days of manufacturing, there was at least one important item to settle. That was the name of my new company. During the early morning I gave thought to that decision. It should be descriptive, easy to say, and with a "ring" to it. Finally, I settled on Taxsaver Company. I liked it, and those I showed it to agreed. So that was my new name. Having made that decision, I set about registering with Internal Revenue Service and the state for required identification numbers. I opened a bank account in the name of Taxsaver Company. I designed stationary and business cards. Very quickly I found myself in business, only awaiting the product and, of course, places to sell them.

One of my clients was a large drug store in town, and I met with them to describe the product and suggest that their store be my inaugeral marketing place. I agreed to place them on consignment, meaning they would not pay until the end of the sales period. I assumed all of the units would be sold, after which I would send an invoice for payment. We not only had an agreement, but they offered to display them on a prominent island for maximum exposure. That was a great offer, I felt, and agreed to provide signs to set up with the display.

As slowly as time can sometimes drag by, the day finally arrived when my Taxsavers were ready for delivery. I had already paid for the kits from my bank loan. I drove down to LA in our station wagon, finally locating the company, and backed up to the loading dock. The manager showed me my kits, and while they really looked black, the interior was just what I had ordered and the quality looked good. I quickly loaded my station wagon with all 500 kits and headed back home. Excitement was mounting with each mile, as I had visions of my kits causing a sensation, calls coming from the store to restock the shelves. My accounting mind calculated the

500 kits @ $3.95 each for a quick $1,975. I would order 500 more at my cost of $1,075, earning another quick $900.00 with each new order.

Arriving back in Santa Maria, I drove directly to the drug store and unloaded my kits on the awaiting island. I had made a couple of signs to set with them, showing a price of $3.95 each. Finally leaving the store, I could not wait to return each day to count the sales and discuss plans with the manager for the best time to reorder.

The next afternoon arrived and I returned to count the missing boxes that had been sold. To my surprise, however, they were all still there, intact. Not a kit was gone! I asked the manager, who said to give it more time as it was a new product. The next day, and the next, I returned to the same result. Something was not right, I thought. This is a busy place. How can this be, or was I counting wrong.? The whole first week passed with no sales, then the second week. During the third week one was sold. By the end of that week the manager asked if I would remove them as there obviously was no interest by customers, and they needed the island for other merchandise. Nearly numb in shock, I loaded them in the car and drove them home. During the ensuing tax season I gave one to each of my tax clients. Eventually, I placed them in a storage shed on our property.

Not to give up on my project that I considered a great one, I drove to Los Angeles, out to Wilshire Blvd., where there were a number of banks and Savings & Loan companies. I visited each, suggesting they buy them for their customers for a promotional item. After all the turndowns I finally drove back home in disgust, admitting to myself that there was obviously something wrong that had caused a well thought out plan to end in failure. But what was it that went wrong? Lets go to the next chapter to look at the facts.

Taxsaver - What went wrong? How could it have been successful?

Let's begin with the color! Black!
Who will have an immediate interest in an all black box?

1. I will readily admit to this error in design, which, in retrospect, was just a small thought, while my focus was all on the interior. How good it was! How much it was needed! But as history showed, no one wanted to even open the box!

2. <u>Marketing:</u> I believe it can be said without hesitation that a marketing specialist was needed. The product would have been studied from the view point of customer appeal, which, of course, would include an attractive exterior. My accounting mind could be no match for a marketing mind.

Here is what might have happened – with professional help.

If I had budgeted for and then found a good marketing specialist, he/she would have listened to my plan and studied my prototype to gain a thorough understanding of what I wanted to do. Their thought process would not have been so much as a tax preparer, as mine was, but as a potential buyer who needed to be carefully attracted enough to at least look at the product, and then decide about purchasing.

They no doubt would have begun work on an attractive exterior for ways to make it attractive. They would have studied the marketplace and planned the best ways to reach it. They probably would have contacted major wholesalers to determine the degree of interest in the product. This important step would precede any production orders. If positive feedback was received then it would be the time to decide whether to go ahead with the project.

They would oversee production of the kits to be certain the final product was as intended. While waiting for production, the media would be called in to plan for appropriate advertising. That would set the stage to create a receptive market when the kits arrived. A major event might be planned to finally introduce Taxsaver to the public, making it available for sale, probably at an introductory price.

With this type of professional planning, sales could have been off to a fabulous start, with growing markets almost assured. My good idea plus the help of experts to run with it would have made the difference to make this venture a huge success!

II.

Glassbath –

It was early in 1968 when one of my clients called me for an appointment. John, a manager of one of the space shuttle projects at Vandenberg Air Force Base, seldom had time to come in, so I felt it was pretty important. Little did I know that a new giant income venture was coming my way. This was one that would virtually change my life and that of my family.

When John arrived we went straight to the point of his visit. Here is the story as he told it. Part of his work dealt with a joint missile launch program with a British team. The director of the UK team had pulled him aside yesterday with this story of a commercial glass washing machine used in bars throughout the UK. One of them was even in Buckingham Palace. In fact, he said it was just about the standard method of washing bar glasses in England. The Company, known as Clean a Glass, had serious interest in establishing a US franchise, and asked the director if he had contacts that would be willing to accept a franchise for the entire US. The director in turn, asked John if he would be interested. It would require establishing retail dealers in key cities throughout the country, to purchase the machines at wholesale and resell in their regions.

A brief description of the machine is that it had the appearance of a glass globe, with three rotating brushes in sanitizing water. As the brushes swirl, the glasses are placed down on them briefly, cleaned and ready for use. The objective is that these machines would replace the three sink method currently being used, because of their efficiency, space saving and more attractive appearance.

Well, this was what the British company was interested in selling to millions of establishments throughout our country. John was drawn to the idea , but his work as an engineer in the space program would not allow much time for such an undertaking. He had discussed the program with a friend, a fellow engineer, and they both were excited about the possibilities. The reason for his visit, he finally revealed, was to suggest that a three way company be formed to take on the franchise. The key to it would be if I would be willing to take the ball as president and devote full time to forming a company and heading up operations. He said he and the other engineer, Zack, would invest funds to purchase the machines from London, and sales would provide rapid capital to cover reorders, my salary and overhead. He suggested a salary for me of $3,000 monthly, to be increased as the company grew. In addition, I would receive stock options to acquire more shares. But it would be my responsibility to negotiate a franchise with England, set up franchises and run company operations. I felt they were offering me a whale of a deal, as the salary was very good in the Sixties. It would of course, be a huge undertaking to establish dealerships, and distribute machines as they arrived, and manage the entire company. . For that kind of money and potential opportunity I felt I could do it. .

There were questions to be answered, due diligence, to ascertain the soundness of such an undertaking. We needed to know the downsides, such as tariffs that could prove prohibitive. Also, acceptance of the machines by the US health department and meeting electrical standards.. For starters, I suggested a meeting of the three of us to go over the entire offer, and to go over plans with great care.

The meeting was held, and as we three discussed details, I recall that we became increasingly enthused about profits and potential growth. To continue a follow through we requested that the British principals come over to discuss the details. It wasn't long before such a meeting took place, with the general manager of Clean a Glass and the British sales manager attending. We met at the Vandenberg Hotel in Santa Maria, where they had set up a machine to demonstrate.. I'll admit, I was taken in by the swirling brushes and efficiency. Finally, getting to the bottom line, we signed an agreement to accept the franchise in return for actively marketing the product. For me personally, this meant devoting full time, which meant no further time for my accounting practice. I took the giant step and met with a local CPA over lunch at the Santa Maria Club. By the end of our lunch, we shook hands on an agreement that I would receive $50,000 in return for turning over my clientele and assisting with the transition. Within a few days we signed an agreement of sale, after which a check was paid to me. Just as quickly as that I was out of the accounting business, one that I had built from scratch over the past seven years. It was like crossing over a bridge from one life to another! But excitement for the new deal moved me forward with renewed energy and resolve to form a great new company.

I recall a jubilant grand opening in my office, previously my accounting office, but now the national headquarters of Glassbath, Inc., the name we gave to our American company. On that day, September 1, 1968, a machine with swirling brushes was easily the focus of attention. The celebration began with a ribbon-cutting ceremony by the Mayor, small speeches, and toasts to the new company in town. My partners and I stood proudly by as we accepted the good wishes of the town dignitaries.

Having formally launched our new company, it was time to go to work. A few key steps were to be taken, following the formation of our new company. One was to apply for the seal of approval from the National Sanitation Foundation, located in Ann Arbor, Michigan. I was soon there, along with a Glassbath machine, and observed the process of examination in the laboratories. Results came by the day's end, when they gave an approval subject to two changes. One was to use a new style brush that would meet US standards, and the other was to get a higher quality sanitizing fluid. Well, that gave us a couple of new hurdles to go over, but we quickly contacted a chemical company to develop the brushes and fluid to meet NSF standards.

Meanwhile, we sent a machine to the UL labs for approval of the electrical system. This test was passed without a problem, giving the approval to attach a UL sticker to each machine.

Turning our attention to marketing, I contacted companies in several cities.

I can no longer recall how we located the contacts, but can say there was a huge amount of interest by potential dealers. They recognized the upgraded cleaning process as revolutionary, and they were eager to join the new wave of glass cleaning. I particularly recall an amazing celebration of a new dealership in

Monterey, held at the elegant Casa Munras Hotel. We arranged for radio and TV coverage of the event, to include dinner and cocktails for all. A new machine was of course, swirling in the adjacent bar, with the bartender proudly demonstrating its use.

We closed the celebration on a high note, giving an interview to the news reporter and wishing the dealership well. It was an evening that seemed to reflect in grand style the beginning of a new venture that was to enjoy vast success and profits. Within the coming weeks I would report to my partners that distributors had been set up in San Francisco, Oakland, Seattle, Los Angeles, Phoenix and even back in Princeton, NJ. It wasn't long before we received out first shipment of 36 machines from Clean a Glass. Huge excitement reigned as profits were felt in each machine we unpacked. I recall one report from a San Francisco airport lounge about the thrill of operating the machine, and time saving during their busy periods. A great improvement over the old method!

And so the business of Glassbath USA flourished for at least two months following the initial delivery of machines. That was about the time we received our first call of a problem. Recall that new brushes were required by the NSF labs, as well as a new detergent. We had of course, followed through by having a chemical company in Los Angeles develop them for us. But while we had approval; it soon became painfully apparent that the brushes and fluid were not compatible! The detergent was causing a gradual disintegration of the rubber brushes. The rubber was beginning to rub off on the glasses, leaving red rings on them. To make matters worse, the rings continued to grow until they were so unsightly the bartender was forced to disband the machine and go back to the old method.

When we received the call from Oakland, we jumped on the phone to the chemical company about fixing the problem - fast! They tested and tested more, with no immediate results. Of course, there was another issue here.. The brushes and sanitizer were approved by the NSF labs. If something new was to replace them, the approval process would have to be repeated again, all the while delaying the correction for dealers. Word was sent over to Clean a Glass. With alarm, they sent a specialist over to investigate and possibly assist the chemical company in finding answers. Their attempts, however, failed to be of any help.

It wasn't long before a second call came with the same problems from Phoenix. It was soon followed by calls from other dealers, all with the same complaint of glasses being ruined by red rings. What had begun with a single call now grew into a crisis, a national crisis for us, and with no immediate fix! Days went by with the chemical company testing and reporting no answer.

The next shock was the return of a defective machine. It was followed by others. Dealers, who had visions of huge profitable business, were now cancelling agreements on the basis of breach of contract. We had failed to perform as agreed. Good feelings of teamwork in this great venture disappeared overnight We obviously failed to perform, and to our grief, we had to admit we were all washed up!

Glassbath - what went wrong?

The introduction of this product to the US market appears to be a great idea. That much we can say was good about Glassbath. Nothing else!

Fish out of water! That is what we can say about three individuals with no knowledge of the bar business, or of mechanics to understand and service the machine, or of marketing. What they did know was only about the profits that could be earned. Two engineers and an accountant (me!).

There had been no mention of a specialist who could understand the machine, how it worked and how to service it when needed. This was an intricate machine with moving parts, electrical systems, a chemical system dispensing fluids in a precise manner . None of the three of us knew anything about it!

Here is what might have happened - with professional help:

The three of us would have begun by preparing a budget for at least the next six months, causing us to look ahead to what we would encounter, and it would have opened our eyes to reality. One thing was to understand our product – the swirling brushes in sanitizing water. Did any of us really know how it worked? Well, it obviously meant we would need a specialized mechanic who would understand it, and would be able to fix problems as they arose.

Secondly, we would have realized we needed a marketing expert, specializing in the restaurant and bar industry, to professionally plan our introduction to the vast U.S. market. There would no doubt have been a regional test period, to test the machine as well as customer satisfaction. At this level, problems arising would be addressed until a smooth operation was assured.

A media expert would likely be retained to plan an effective announcement of the revolutionary machine; also, a grand opening to introduce it to the public.

Each of the specialists would have been costly, but realizing a national franchise was in our hands, a budget commensurate with our goals was definitely warranted. Having created our budget to include the professional help needed, we would be in a position to calculate the funds needed and plan fund raising. If we had no solution to fund raising, then it would mean that we were not in a position to undertake the project.

Our budget would have been large, but resulting sales would likely have repaid the cash outlay, with earnings potentially, and very likely in the millions. The key here is that professional planning and execution of the plans would have made the difference, turning our venture into the huge success we envisioned.

III.

The Dawn of Personal Computers - - PSI, Inc.

Most of us can recall somewhere in our lifetime when a "window of opportunity" opened for us. It was that time when you could embark on a new pathway that held the potential for great things to happen if all went well. If ever there was such an "opening" in my life, this was it. I can't wait to tell you about it.

It was in the Spring of 1974, when I went to one of my accounting clients, an office equipment store in Santa Barbara. There were normally rows of typewriters on display, but this time a new item stood out like a bold headline. It was my first ever viewing of a personal computer!

Back in 1957 I had taken a class on computers at UCLA, when an entire room had been built to house the big unit. Temperatures were controlled to maintain constant conditions. But on this day a small unit, slightly larger than a typewriter was there, with no need for special temperatures or other conditions. It was amazing to behold, I can tell you that! I believe the main reasons I felt that way was because I was able to visualize the applications that would allow hundreds , even thousands of faster ways to calculate and maintain business records. It would apply to every company in the world. It would quickly out perform the old calculator and even the typewriter. This was almost too exciting to believe! Since our class in the 1950's, I had guessed the time would come one day, but I had no idea it would be here on this day. It was right here, and as history has shown us, the world has become a vastly different place, all because of this revolutionary personal computer.

Even as I examined the PC, some very personal ideas came to me about its application in accounting. I believed it held the potential for a first ever computerized accounting machine. There could be separate keys for journals, then keys to post the journals into the general ledger, another for general journal entries, and finally a key to punch out a financial statement. I will say, It was an exciting day for me to see the existence of the first ever PC.

It was only a few weeks after visiting the store when a second amazing event took place. Two men came to my office, introducing themselves as computer engineers, sent from the office equipment store. The owners knew of my special interest in the PC, and suggested that they should go to see me. They explained that they were presently employed at nearby Vandenberg Air Force Base, writing software programs for various military applications. However, their real interest lay in forming a company to develop programs for commercial uses. They had taken that first step already by forming PSI, Inc.. In fact, in their spare time they had begun working on a program relating to the travel industry.

In those days all travel preparations for ticketing were accomplished by telephone. An agent would call the airline, usually having to wait on "hold" to speak to someone. The time involved to complete ticketing and prepare an invoice was normally as much as one-half hour. The objective of the new software being written by these two gentlemen was to accomplish this task within a fraction of the time.

Why had they come to me, I questioned? Well, they explained that they knew what they were doing, but knew nothing about operating a business. The office equipment people had recommended me as someone who could help them. They needed financial guidance, personnel to be hired, assistance in raising operating funds, and generally running the business while they remained focused on their development work. Their question was whether I would be willing to help them.

So here was a new opportunity. My thoughts immediately went back a few years to my Glassbath fiasco, and the disaster it had created for my family. I would learn from that, while continuing my accounting practice. I believed I could take on this project as another client. I knew of a larger space I could move to, large enough for a laboratory to be located next to my office. Learning from my past mistakes, I felt this plan would be entirely feasible. A substantial increase in my income would be welcomed by my family, and we could once again look to the future with new hope and excitement. I recalled that in 1974, in a garage a few hundred miles North, Steve Jobs and his partner were also starting up a small enterprise. They were known by my soon to be associates, Homer Tilley and his fellow software pioneers. Those were truly the "early days" as we were to be a part of the new wave! It was nearly too exciting to comprehend!

With those immediate reactions, along with the promise once again of increased income and stock options, I accepted their offer. Within a few weeks we had moved into our new quarters and their lab was in full swing. Adjacent to my office, they worked tirelessly to program each phase of our travel program. Before long they were actually building a modem. This was a required device to interphase with the travel center. They eventually accomplished this vital connection, something that seemed to me comparable with the first telephone contact. Homer and I developed the habit of meeting for a few minutes each morning to discuss progress and plan ahead for future needs. Our prevailing need for much of the time was operating funds to pay salaries, utilities, etc. I had applied for a Small Business loan at my bank. My bank manager listened to my description of our company project and future plans with growing enthusiasm, but had to tell me that, due to the early stages of the industry, my application would be carefully studied, probably taking longer than usual to reach approval. That was understandable, and I was encouraged by his comments, saying that he felt a great future lay ahead for our company and the computer industry. Meanwhile, I attempted to raise funds by selling shares of company stock and by loans with a higher than normal interest rate. I was actually quite successful in raising funds in this way. In fact, a manager at another bank in town said his bank could not approve a loan due to the infancy of the computer industry, but he personally would loan his money, to be converted to stock at a later time. No doubt, many who were aware of the breakthrough in the developing PC were convinced as I was, that it was the wave of the future.

Day by day small progress was made, and the months flew by. One day the salesman for the office equipment store stopped by, explaining that he would like to take on our travel program as a part of his product line. In fact, he revealed, he had spoken to a travel agent in nearby Goleta about our development. He had received an enthusiastic response by the agent, who said he would like to come by and see our developing product. We responded affirmatively, and had ourselves a salesman! It was not long before a second travel agent heard of our product and expressed serious interest. This was the growing atmosphere in which our program was nearing completion.

We were closing in on the Spring of 1975 when my lab people announced that they had a working system. Some final testing was needed, and it would be ready for sale! None too soon as funds were running out to pay wages and overhead.. Arrangements were made with each of the two travel offices to deliver the systems. The price for each was $16,500, cash on delivery. It was in mid-May when the first system was installed, with the new owner standing by proudly like a new father. Success! Contact was made with an airline and a transaction was nicely completed. Only a few days later the second system was installed at office number two!! Second success! It was truly a euphoric feeling to watch our lab people and the new owners work together in operating the system. There was so much pride and unbounded excitement in watching this new breakthrough in the scientific world.

That was when our windows of opportunity in the dawning of PC's came crashing down, with not one more system to be sold. American Airlines announced the arrival of the Sabre System, a program nearly identical to ours. The vast difference, however,, was that it was introduced with a marketing program that we could never match. Terms of sale were for over a two year installment period. Also, a three day all expenses paid visit to a resort location was offered for training of the operators.. And not of the least importance was the established name of American Airlines.

Their announcement reached every sales office, and was obviously well received. As our salesman visited offices he was greeted with the news of the new offer from American, and "no thanks" to our amazing system.

Our company, while at the advent of incredible success, found itself dead in the water! A great product, but no further sales. Logic said we could begin a new software program, but funds had run out. The SBA loan had not yet been approved, and the technicians were burned out. They had given all they had, and were in a state of shock at being suddenly out sold by American. They left. Our company, that only a few weeks earlier, was ready to fly to the moon, had crash landed. It was over!

The Dawn of Personal Computers – PSI, Inc. - What went Wrong?

First, let's see what was right about the project.

Timing could not have been better. 1975 was the year when the PC was introduced to a market that had been waiting, and was hungry for its arrival.

PC's, short for personal computers, were, of course, a natural for every household user. They were also perfect for commercial uses. Now that the technology was available, the most desired addition was software. Applications, now known as apps, were needed for every imaginable purpose. That was the very reason PSI, Inc. existed.

Our technical know-how was also perfect. We had two very sharp engineers, experienced in developing software for military purposes, and amazingly capable of writing software programs with the "unfriendly" language in use at that time.

Our first project of building a travel program was as good as any other. Almost any commercial app would have been perfect because there were none available.

So what went wrong? How could it have been a success?

If ever there was an undertaking destined for success, this was it, but we would need to take a few smart steps to make it happen. Here is what we might have done:

First, and most importantly, would be to prepare a budget, one that recognized and planned for obvious needs. The needs would include salaries for personnel, cost of materials needed in the project, and other overhead expenses. Also to include the cost of specialists, to be explained below.

Secondly, we knew there was a desperate need for our type of product, software programs, but we should have realized that there were others who would literally be working day and night to fill those needs. In other words, competition would be growing to do exactly what we were doing. Timing would be of the essence, and also legal protection. We would retain a marketing specialist with an understanding of the computer industry and potential customers who would need our services.

We would retain a sharp attorney, knowledgeable in contracts to develop working agreements with major companies to provide our expertise. In other words, we would be retained by specific firms to produce the software they needed. Most specifically, we would have contacted the airlines, advising of the software being prepared for their industry. At lease one airline would no doubt commit by contract to deal with us and use our program.

Once these steps were taken, we would be in a position to include costs of our experts in the budget. We would also be in a position to include income as pre-payments from those companies under contract as income.

A vast advantage would have been gained at this stage. We would have arranged for assured, prepayments as income, and have established our company as a presence, a force in the new software industry. Instead of working quietly and unknown in our lab, we would have made our company known in the emerging computer world. Success in this billion dollar industry would have been a certainty if we had taken a few smart moves in the beginning.

IV.

An Agent in Egypt

Here is an actual business experience that took on world-wide proportions during the Summer of 1980. Having suffered the heartbreak in 1975, when our personal computer venture was suddenly shattered by American Airlines, I managed to regroup. We had since moved to Reno, Nevada, and I entered the real estate profession to augment income from a few accounting clients.

It was a real estate client who asked me to visit him in his home, as he had some business to discuss. Assuming we would discuss the purchase or sale of property, I readily agreed. Upon arriving, I was warmly greeted by Mike and his charming wife. They had a very comfortable home, well appointed, but not excessively.

We soon began our discussion of his special interest, and to my surprise, it had nothing to do with real estate. Mike began by describing his background, mostly in his country of birth, Egypt. He grew up in Cairo, receiving his education at the University of Cairo, and emigrated to the United States in his early twenties. He explained that he had many friends and good business contacts throughout the Middle-Eastern countries, through his fathers business. Of particular interest was that most of those contacts were in governmental positions of influence.

Now, to the point of this meeting, he brought up the recent event of the Camp David Accord, arranged by President Jimmy Carter, that had the objective of bringing about peace between Israel and Egypt. The timing was perfect, Mike explained, to use his contacts while promoting trade between those countries. Farming equipment was sorely needed, as well as technical equipment, aircraft and many other industrial items. He went on to say that he felt he had come to know me during our dealings in real estate, and he believed we would be an excellent team to travel to the Middle-East and become brokers, or agents in bringing together dozens of transactions. On each we would earn a healthy commission that we would split equally. Well, I'll have to say, I never expected an offer like this! The prospects sounded enormous, in worldly proportions that could earn literally millions for us as the agents between the two countries.

Mike offered to team up with me for about two to three months, travelling during the Summer months of 1980. We would probably visit the United Emirates, Saudi Arabia, Morocco,,, and of course, Egypt. If I agreed to such a trip, we could begin meeting in his home once weekly to carefully plan the trip. He further suggested that we share expenses equally, which he estimated at about $20,000. As I listened, his descriptions actually sounded surreal, like a story I might read in a book. But, of course, I realized he was speaking to me, and that if I agreed, we could be travelling across the world in just a matter of months. I could see strange lands and meet people in far away places, bring them together in huge financial transactions, and come home with wealth that I had been seeking for so many years.

I replied that I would give it serious thought and let him know in a few days. Not wanting to appear too blown away by it all, I explained it would take some thought as to my present time commitments, finances and other matters.

Of course, the prospects of such an amazing trip presented a huge attraction for me for starters. All of the earnings he described definitely overshadowed any doubts I might have had. I made a decision to tentatively agree, subject to attending our first few meetings to learn more about Mike and the substance of his ideas. I believed those meetings would allow me to evaluate him and his ability to carry out the plans he described. These thoughts were what I related to Mike, as we began our weekly meetings. With each meeting, I became more impressed with his knowledge of the countries and the specific contacts we would make, one actually being the president of Morocco. With each meeting I become more convinced that our project would be successful, and eventually agreed to his terms by giving him a letter of consent.

The month of May arrived, and my travels began with a brief stop in Washington, D.C. to obtain visas from the embassies of the countries we planned to visit. With success on this first day, we continued on to London, where Mike took me to an excellent Arabian restaurant, that I might have a taste of Middle-Eastern dining. Following this short stop we headed South to begin our work.

On our arrival in Cairo I was immediately hit with the reality of our mission. Here we were in this ancient city of thirteen million inhabitants, hustling about their daily chores as they no doubt have done for centuries. As I arrived at my hotel room on the thirteenth floor, I stepped out on the balcony. Just a short distance away was the mighty Nile, flowing swiftly along to end its journey to the Mediterranean. I could see countless Arabs in their white robes on their way to the outdoor market place a short distance away. Well, I was thrilled to be in this strange land for awhile, and was ready to begin our work.

We began our first day by taking a taxi downtown, where we entered an ancient building, taking an equally ancient elevator to the third floor, where we met Abaza.

He was a short, middle aged Arab, who would be our agent while we were here. I had learned that anyone in Egypt for business purposes must have an agent. Mike apparently knew him well, and our meeting was a lively one, thankfully all in English. Abaza described our goals as timely,, due to the improved relations with Israel. He followed that comment with an enthusiastic reference to a project for us. He explained that a local citizen owned a parcel of land bordering the Nile, on which he planned to build a nine story five star hotel. He would donate his land to a new development company as his share of equity. Further, Abaza explained, two French investors were seriously interested in investing and becoming developers of the property. He suggested that Mike and I might act as coordinators and administrators of the project, a position that would be worth several millions. The timing was right, he said, as the Cairo government had just given approval of the project.

Well, this situation sounded perfect to Mike. He said we could take it on while moving ahead with the other contacts. While it sounded quite spectacular and lucrative to me, I wondered just how much we could accomplish during our 2-3 month stay in Cairo. Mike replied, "No worry, we will have a great start and earn a huge fee while here.". He was eager to meet the French investors, and so we did on the following day.

I recall sitting with Mike, Abaza and the Frenchmen, where a lively, animated discussion took place, partly in French, partly in Arabic and also English. An amazing experience! It sounded to me about as international as it could be. Frequently, Mike would explain to me what had been discussed. Before long, I was taking notes about potential sales of the completed hotel, construction costs, operating expenses and profits. Also, we discussed a financing program that consisted of the landowners land value to be invested, the French investment, the amount of local bank financing available, and finally the remaining amount required to move ahead with the project. There were a few million dollars more required to complete funding the program, and it appeared that we, Mike and I, would be responsible to locaate investors for the additional amount.

Following the meeting, far up in my hotel room, I began analyzing the entire program. In order to make it available to all parties, I had columns for each language, converting into American dollars, English pounds (used in Egypt) and French francs. , a formidable task that was a first for me. I will admit, my figures showed the project to be an excellent investment. Much as it appeared desirable to me, I was most concerned about our ability to earn our share during the short time of our visit. I later questioned Mike as to whether this was the right project for us. It held great promise for earnings , but it was obviously a long-term project. Did it fit with the plans we had made in advance? He quickly responded that it was far better than anything we had planned on, and that we could do this , plus some of the other deals too. In fact, he mentioned that he would be leaving for a few days on a trip to Morocco, where he would make arrangements for our meeting there a short time later. During his absence, my job was to lay out the planning for our Hotel on the Nile for presentation to potential investors upon his return.

During the three day period Mike was gone I did my best to formulate a presentation of the hotel project. It was similar to some I had prepared while in Santa Barbara, except for the conversion to three currencies. I'll admit, it did look like an excellent investment in terms of cash flow and equity build. After working steadily for two days, I decided that I 'd earned a break, and I knew exactly how I would spend it. Only a short walking distance from my hotel room stood the legendary pyramids of Giza, and also the mighty Sphinx . I decided to take advantage of this lifetime opportunity, and began my exciting walk.

Well, in a very short time I was there, attempting to place myself in the saddle of a stubborn camel. Finally, I was in place and we began a most amazing trip around all three of the giant structures. How I wished for more time to spend walking even closer, and maybe climbing up the giant rocks as some people were doing, and maybe even exploring one of tunnels leading inside the pyramid. But as I was, up on my camel, it was awesome and most exciting. Following that trip I took an unforgettable visit into a structure beside the pyramid. Called a Mastaba, as explained by a scruffy looking Arab, it was used to hold the less important royalty, while the most important were buried in the pyramids. I agreed to follow my self-appointed guide down underground, down a small tunnel at about 45 degrees. Behind me was another scruffy bearded Arab, who described the unbelievable hyroglifics and the sarcafigus holding an ancient mummy . It was truly a site to remember. All of this was shown to me at a price, of course, and as I paid them a few pounds and retraced my steps up the tunnel, I felt as though I was escaping to freedom. I soon passed the big toe of the Sphinx and headed back to my hotel room, with so much to think about. I thought to myself on that night, "if nothing turns out of our financial adventure, at least I will always remember this night at one of the ancient wonders of the world! Well, to shorten my story, that is exactly what happened. I'll explain shortly.

The focus of our daily activities continued to stay on the hotel project, with potential investors being introduced to us. We met several in the lobby of our hotel, where it seemed to be the custom to transact business. At most any time of the day, small groups could be seen, some becoming animated, while others appeared to be cloaked in quiet secrecy. One of my meetings developed quite successfully. A gentleman from Abbu Dabi listened quietly to the presentation, and said he was impressed with it. He would do his "due diligence", or detailed study of the numbers and property, and if found to be as presented, he would invest. As our discussion was ending another amazing moment occurred. He offered me an excellent position at a substantial income if I would agree to move to Abbu Dabi and work for him in his company. That was a most gratifying thought but not in the cards for me. We agreed to remain in touch about the hotel project and parted on good terms.

Other meetings were less hopeful, but we continued on, without any other projects being started. The more I pressed Mike on the other areas of our work, the more he insisted, with agitation, that the hotel project would be successful, and was the best way to spend our time.

As June passed into July, and eventually into August, I observed the actions of Mike with increasing scrutiny. It became abundantly clear to me that he was not interested in other projects. He was, in fact, lying to me on a number of occasions. I discovered that a great deal of time was spent just visiting with his brothers and sisters, all of whom lived in Cairo. I just recently learned by chance that his trip to "Morocco" had not taken place, but that he had actually flown back to the United States to visit with his family. After that revelation, I was convinced that he had planned the entire trip on my funds in order to visit his family. He was a complete fraud, of that I was finally convinced .I told him that directly, and he stormed out of the room, never to be seen by me again.

We were never able to complete the hotel program, due in part to the shortness of time, and of course, our inability to work together after his fraudulent scheme was uncovered. And there were no "other projects", of that I felt sure. I returned home, having to explain to my family how Mike was a fraud, and that, instead of bringing riches with me, my pockets were empty!

Agents in Egypt - - - What went wrong?

I have no doubt that fortunes were made by some, following the Camp David Accord of 1979. But it was not to happen for me, due to at least three huge errors in planning.

My first error was in not checking into the background of my partner, to learn what kind of a scoundrel he was. He spoke well, in fact, most impressively, as many unscrupulous crooks often do. Knowing the Middle-East, he was able to talk about it in ways that were fascinating and exciting.

As a result, I was blinded by the riches to be made, It all sounded logical, and as something we could certainly do, given his contacts. But all the time, money and grief of defeat could have been saved by finding out just who he was in advance.

Secondly, by insisting on actual communication with the contacts he spoke of, to ascertain their validity and actual interest in meeting with us, would have built strong support for the program. As it was, they were actually fictional.

Finally, the moral of this fascinating but sad story is to avoid at all costs by being blinded by the prospect of huge riches in the future. Check out details in advance, and search for flaws in the offer. Be pessimistic until proven otherwise. Insist on full disclosure of any and all details, including finances. When resistance is found, push harder to uncover the reasons. When the reasons are difficult to uncover, they should be the reasons to say no to the deal.

V.

Real Estate Reports and Seminars –

Shortly after returning from my fiasco in Egypt, I was doing everything possible to recover. My family of eight required my support more than ever, continuing the pressure for producing a steady income.

By 1980 the advent of computers was taking the entire world by storm, with IBM, Microsoft and Apple producing hardware and software at a record pace. I still wanted to be a part of it all, and while I did not understand programming very well, I could appreciate the amazing benefits of completed programs.

I joined the parade of computer types by developing a plan for analyzing income producing property. My accounting background helped greatly in laying out all the needed steps. The data about a specific property needed gathering, including rental income, associated expenses, amount of investment, total cost, depreciation and a few other details. All of this data had to be entered into the program, and once entered, the amazing machine would calculate the return on investment that a buyer might earn. It was an excellent tool to be used by a seller in determining the best selling price that would provide a good earnings for an investor. I was truly proud of my creation, and what it could mean for the real estate industry.

Once completed on paper, I located a programmer, that is, an individual who could prepare the program in a computer using computer language. I paid him $3,000 to prepare the program, a task that I could do in Excel today in about an hour. But those were the "early days", when specialists who knew computer language were in high demand.

I tested my new program in an actual situation, with a property that had been on the market for $215,000 without an offer for the past six months. Preparing my report of the property, I gave it to the owners, who showed it to an interested party. The report indicated a selling price of $265,000, higher than the original price by $50,000. The property sold in two days! Well, I knew I had a good product, one that would be extremely useful in the commercial real estate industry. I further supported the report by preparing a manual with which a report could also be prepared manually, without having to enter the data into a computer.

To begin marketing my program, I prepared introductory material, sending it to the commercial real estate department of every real estate office in Reno. Incidentally, the cost of publishing the manual and preparing two hundred copies was about $5,000. That cost , together with my earlier programming fee, brought my investment in the project to over $8,000.

The result of my promotional campaign was that I did not receive a single reply! I could not believe it! What would it take to get my idea across that this was a valuable assist to their work as commercial real estate people.? It was something that would help them to earn commissions.

I followed up my mailings with a few personal visits to the offices that had not responded to my mail. I met with a few of the commercial real state people, and believed I learned what the problems was. It seemed that while the world was moving well into the computer age, the realtors still did not understand what it meant to use a computer program. It seemed to be more than they could deal with, which of course, required a departure from their present methods of selling. Because they could not understand it, they did not buy it. Simple as that !

Seminars:
Even though my first entry into the market did not go well, I was as convinced as ever that my program was good. When understood, it could become a huge success, but not yet. I was determined as ever to use it, and my next idea was to prepare a seminar for real estate personnel. With this approach, I could describe the program and the benefits of using it. The presentation of seminars was becoming a huge industry in itself, being presented to professional groups, including medical, law, accounting and real estate. Renewal of professional licenses required credits that could be earned by attending seminars, so I felt that that I could fit in perfectly by providing one of my own.

I first prepared a lesson plan that required approval and certification by the State departments of Education, and it was accepted. I selected a town in the California Central Valley of Hanford. I had a good friend there who owned an airplane, and he offered to fly me from Reno to Hanford and return. That, of course, was a huge help, as it saved about a day of driving.

My seminar was attended by 40 realtors, each paying $45 and receiving four education credits. I received some fine reviews, indicating that I had a good program. Returning home with earnings of $1,800, I was finally pleased with my latest source of earnings.

However, when analyzing the first presentation and the prospect of presenting more, I had to face the true facts. The first fact was that, to develop a continuing series of seminars required more than just myself. Time was a key factor, requiring time to promote, to prepare, print and coordinate all promotional and class materials, and to schedule locations in cities throughout Nevada and California. That was a full time job for one person. Time again was the important factor in travelling to each city, always with a new supply of books and other materials for the attendees. At least one very efficient employee was needed, two would be even better to assist me at each seminar site.

Considering the time to travel to each city, the cost of staying overnight and paying wages would net out at a much lower net income. And that was assuming an attendance of at least forty at each program. I did not know of anyone I could hire for the job, and in truth did not have backup funds in the event earnings fell off. In the end, I was enthused about the entire seminar program, but had to admit it was more than I alone could handle. My company ended with my first seminar.

Real Estate Reports and Seminars -- What went wrong?

Looking first at the good side:

- I believe the plan of presenting a good seminar was an excellent idea. Programs as mine were part of a substantial industry expanding across the country. They were popular and accepted methods of learning in the professions, as well as the source of education credits for license renewals. I had done my homework by preparing a quality, certified seminar.

How it might have succeeded:

Once again, a carefully prepared budget was needed, to include all costs to be incurred to make the program operate smoothly.

By planning for a full-time person who would prepare materials needed for each seminar, schedule programs in advance, locate and pay rent for locations and arrange for my overnight stay, I believed it would be a workable program. Now those costs could be included in the budget.

On the positive side of the budget, we would estimate the average number of attendees at each program, and the income to be earned.. This would be the most difficult part, but we might come close by using conservative figures. Once entered, we would be in a position to study the budget as a whole.

I would want to determine if my program appeared to be profitable. This would be the critical time to decide, before committing to seminar dates. If it was not, or close to a break-even, then we would know if we should proceed or not, saving our time for a more profitable venture.

How I survived five failures –

There was a certain valuable element that I possessed as I literally plunged into each new venture. With my intense motivation to earn the "big money", to provide for my family, I managed to overlook the fact that I was a successful accountant.

Accounting was my strong suit, my strength. It was a profession I had learned well, and proved my ability as I built a large clientele in Santa Maria over a relatively short time. In fact, if I had stopped to realize these facts, instead of taking on ventures that I knew very little about, in which I was a novice, I would have known that in due time my accounting firm would have grown large enough to support my family. And, of course, I could have remained in Santa Maria instead of being forced out.

A close review of my accounting practice reveals these facts:

- Accounting was my strong suit. I was not the unskilled novice that I became when trying to manage the five companies that failed.

- I did not require additional working capital to operate, as there was no inventory or other hidden cost to pay for. My present income was sufficient to pay for overhead. In fact, my company was always profitable.
- I had no need to rely on partners, as in the Agent in Egypt venture.
- Travel was not required.

Those were powerful assets that I somehow overlooked when jumping into the unknown waters in each of the companies that eventually failed.

As I went from one venture to the next, I actually continued to provide accounting services that brought in a stream of income, even though meager for my needs. Eventually, when my five company failures became history, I continued in my accounting profession, becoming the controller for two large companies.

My advice to offer is to play your strong suit. Develop your special skills and stay with them, for they will take you to greater heights in your career, with greater possibilities of success, and vastly greater satisfaction. As other potentially lucrative ventures come your way, plan ahead carefully before taking another step. Prepare a budget and bring in specialists as needed to assist in deciding whether or not to become involved.

Winding Things Up

When I began this book, my goals were to give a hand to every new company owner by passing on all of the best advice I could. Over my years of working with new companies, I've seen many grow in size, strength and earnings, while for one or more reasons, others just did not make it.

My hope is to, as the old song of World War II went: accentuate the positive and eliminate the negatives. I want to point you in the direction of preserving your cash, using it in more productive ways, improving sales, cutting costs and maximizing net profits.

In Part II, I called your attention to some fatal errors I made in my early years. Each was a new company in which I became involved that did not make it. Each story was intended to leave you with a message to remember certain errors to avoid. By all means, avoid them!

Turning to the positive, above all, utilize budgets and cash flow worksheets, plan ahead, apply cash controls. Recall the chapter on using your strong suit and augmenting your management strength by calling on specialists as needed. You may have the winning ideas, and they can help you to implement them. Finally, always believe in yourself, and reinforce your beliefs by knowing your company intimately; know your products, utilize principles discussed in this book, and persevere always.

If you will put into practice the subjects discussed in this book, I will be thrilled with your success.

Wishing you all the best as you build your company and achieve your goals.

Rudy

The best power steps spell cash profits!

The first few steps you will take in your new company, if taken properly, can start you on the road to strength and success. You will want to establish regular procedures that you can grow with, forming habits for controlling your company and reaching your goals. That is what this book is all about.

Cash is your power word, and you will discover the best ways to build cash in your company. Learn the magic of inventory turnover, how to control your receivables, the great value of cash flow analysis and cash projecting, Learn how to use the latest tax changes that affect today's business world. You will learn how to build a strong professional staff to assist you, at no cost to you except when needed.

Unique to this book are five real life, amazing stories about new company ventures with million dollar goals that did not succeed. The author lived these experiences in his early years, and explains the few valued steps that could have changed failure into success. Learn the key moves to avoid while breaking through the barriers toward realizing your goals. Build Your Company for Success will help you to jump far ahead of most new companies with a realistic guide about what to avoid and the key steps to take in building cash reserves and profits. This is a no nonsense, down to earth book about helping to reach your goals, even in our highly competitive business world of today.

www.ingramcontent.com/pod-product-compliance
Lightning Source LLC
Chambersburg PA
CBHW062159220526
45470CB00009B/2873